IT'S A FACT! Real-Life Reads

P9-CSA-464

Your Dog's Superhero Skills

by Ellen Lawrence

Series consultant:

Suzy Gazlay, MA
Recipient, Presidential Award for Excellence in Science Teaching

Ruby Tuesday Books

Published in 2015 by Ruby Tuesday Books Ltd.

Copyright © 2015 Ruby Tuesday Books Ltd.

Editor: Mark J. Sachner
Designer: Emma Randall
Production: John Lingham

Photo Credits:
Alamy: 15, 24–25, 27; Corbis: 11; FLPA: 6–7; Paulette Gooder: 23; Shutterstock: Cover, 4–5, 8–9, 10, 12–13, 14–15, 16–17, 18–19, 20–21, 22, 26, 28–29, 31.

Library of Congress Control Number: 2014957407

ISBN 978-1-909673-86-1

Printed and published in the United States of America

For further information including rights and permissions requests, please contact our Customer Service Department at 877-337-8577.

Contents

A Superhero in Your Home?

Imagine creatures that can sprint alongside a speeding car. Or powerful beings that can run over ice and snow for 100 miles (160 km) without needing to rest.

They have night vision and super hearing. Their hyper-sensitive noses can detect whether a friend or enemy passed through a building today, yesterday, or even the day before.

These creatures may sound like movie or comic-book superheroes. But in fact, we're describing dogs and their incredible senses and skills.

Dogs may not wear masks and capes. But it doesn't mean they can't sniff out danger, capture villains, and even save lives!

Prehistoric Dogs and Wild Wolves

Most dogs love to run, chase, and sniff at everything. The way dogs behave is a clue that our pets were once **predators** that hunted for their food.

So how did wild hunters become our playful pets?

There have been dog-like predators on Earth since prehistoric times.

Over millions of years, these animals **evolved**. They became wolves, coyotes, jackals, and the other wild members of the dog family.

Then, about 20,000 years ago, some wild wolves began living alongside humans. This probably happened in several different places around the world. In time, some wolves became tame, or **domesticated**.

The First Pet Dogs

Scientists don't know for sure how wolves first came to live with ancient humans.

Perhaps some wolves learned they could find scraps of food in villages.

Maybe, just like humans today, our **ancestors** could not resist a cute puppy. It's possible that people captured wild wolf cubs to raise them as pets.

Wolves live in small family groups. They hunt as a team and share food. Older cubs often help take care of younger brothers and sisters. Ancient wild wolves were used to living as part of a wolf family. Perhaps this helped wolves learn how to fit in with a new kind of family—humans!

A gray wolf mother and cub

A gray wolf cub

The Dog Goes to Work

The wild wolves that first lived with humans were the ancient ancestors of our pet dogs.

Dogs enjoy getting attention from people, so they are easy to train. In time, people realized that dogs could be trained to do work.

People bred small dogs to catch rats, rabbits, and other animals that live in holes and burrows.

A small Jack Russell terrier digging in a rabbit hole

Large dogs were bred to guard sheep and goats. Just like wolves that protect their family members, guard dogs think of the sheep as their family.

Over thousands of years, people created hundreds of different dog **breeds**.

This Great Pyrenees dog is guarding sheep to keep them safe from coyotes.

The Superdog Squad

Today, dogs come in many shapes and sizes, with many different skills. Some of their incredible abilities make them seem like movie and comic-book superheroes.

So which of our **canine** friends would we assemble to form…

The Superdog Squad?

SPEED

No dog is faster than the greyhound. In just a few strides, it can reach a speed of 45 miles an hour (72 km/h)!

ENDURANCE

For toughness and **endurance**, it's the sled dog. In temperatures of -10°F (-23°C), these dogs might pull a sled for up to 100 miles (160 km) without a rest.

STRENGTH

Most dogs are strong for their size. Some large bullmastiffs, however, can actually pull loads up to 70 times their own weight!

Night Vision

Dogs can have speed and strength. They also have other super skills. One of them is night vision!

Inside both dogs' and humans' eyes are millions of **cells** called rods. These cells help us see when there is very little light. Dogs' eyes have many more rods than human eyes. Being able to see in dim light helped your dog's wild ancestors hunt at night.

Dogs' eyes also have a mirror-like section called a **tapetum**. When light enters humans' or dogs' eyes, it hits each eye's **retina**. Once light hits a dog's retina, it reflects off the tapetum and hits the retina again. This helps the dog's eyes collect extra light for good night vision.

If a dog looks into light, such as a flashlight beam, the tapetum in its eyes reflects the light. This makes the dog's eyes glow.

Super Ears

Have you ever noticed your dog suddenly seem to freeze? You can't see or hear anything, but your super pooch is on high alert.

It's likely your dog's ears have detected a faraway sound that your ears cannot pick up. A dog's sense of hearing is about four times more sensitive than a human's.

Dogs hear all the same sounds that humans do. They also hear sounds that are too high-pitched for human ears to detect.

Just listening for the mail lady...

A dog's sensitive ears are always on the move. They move to help the dog pinpoint where noises are coming from.

This part of the ear is called the pinna. Most dogs have large pinnae that amplify, or increase, the loudness of sounds.

A World of Smells

Dogs have an incredibly powerful sense of smell. Their wild ancestors needed this super sense for tracking prey.

Today, our dogs still love to sniff. When you go to a park, you might see trees and grass. Your dog will see these things, too. But he will also detect an invisible world of smelly information.

Hey! New girl in town.

Bruce from next door was here.

Using his sensitive nose, your dog might smell other dogs that visited the park yesterday. A squirrel that ran over the grass two days ago. A cat that prowled through the park at midnight. Or a half-eaten hamburger hidden under some leaves.

Drool. I smell hamburger...

A squirrel
A squirrel
A squirrel

Cat!

A Super Nose

Just what makes our dogs' noses so good at smelling?

Inside both human and dog noses there is a part called the **olfactory epithelium** that captures smells.

In a human's nose this part is the size of a postage stamp. In a dog's nose it is much larger. A German shepherd's olfactory epithelium is about the size of a DVD case.

A German shepherd

The olfactory epithelium is covered with receptors that capture smells. Your nose has about 10 million scent receptors. Your dog's nose has about 225 million.

Scientists estimate that a dog's sense of smell is thousands of times more powerful than a human's!

As it follows a scent trail, a dog usually sniffs about six times a second. It can increase its sniff rate, however, to 20 sniffs a second!

A Nose for Saving Lives

Many dogs use their super sense of smell to save lives.

Search and rescue dogs are trained to find lost people.

Dogs can search forests, mountainsides, and other wilderness areas fast. Before setting off, the dog sniffs a piece of clothing that belongs to the lost person. It ignores all other smells and searches for that scent alone.

A person sheds, or loses, about 40,000 dead skin cells every minute. It's this scent trail of skin cells that a search and rescue dog follows.

A search and rescue dog in a desert

A search and rescue team
with dogs on a lake

Sometimes a dog must search for someone who has
drowned in a lake or river. The dog's powerful nose
can detect a person's scent, even when the body is
deep underwater.

Bomb Dogs

Explosive Detection Canines, or bomb dogs, are trained to smell for explosives.

Bomb dogs examine luggage at airports. They search buildings at events where a terrorist might hide a bomb.

In war zones, bomb dogs and their handlers check roadsides and buildings for hidden bombs. Moving fast and sniffing hard, a dog can check a large area in a short time.

Zamp the bomb dog
working with marines
in Afghanistan

Once a bomb dog smells explosives, it usually sits very
still close to its discovery. It is trained not to get excited
because sudden movements could make the bomb explode.

When a bomb dog finds explosives, it gets a reward—a
game with its favorite toy!

Crime Fighters

Police dogs, or K-9s, use their speed, **agility**, strength, and super noses to fight crime.

A suspected criminal is hiding out in a large, dark, empty building. Police officers send in a K-9 to hunt down the culprit.

The dog doesn't need a flashlight. All it needs is its nose! Running at high speed, the dog races through the building. In a flash, it smells a trail of skin cells left by the suspect.

In a fraction of the time it would take officers to search the building, the dog finds the suspect. It barks loudly and keeps the suspect cornered until the police arrive to make an arrest.

When chasing criminals, a K-9 dog may have to leap over high walls, fences, and other objects. Here a police dog demonstrates its agility.

This police dog is practicing catching a suspect who's escaping on a bike!

Superdog

Imagine what it would be like to live with a superhero.

This being would be fast, agile, and strong. It would have night vision and an amazing sense of smell. It would be able to hear sounds that no human could ever detect.

If you share your home with a dog, you don't have to imagine these kinds of powers. Every day, you can see your dog's super skills and senses in action.

Many dogs go to work and face danger every day. Their superhero skills are used to rescue people and fight crime.

Of course, our lovable, playful dogs aren't *really* superheroes.

Able to race a speeding automobile...

Or ARE they?

Glossary

agility (uh-JIL-ih-tee)
The ability to move quickly, easily, and gracefully.
An agile dog might jump up onto a wall, balance
along the wall, and then leap back onto the ground.

ancestor (AN-sess-tur)
A relative who lived a long time ago. For example,
your great-grandparents and great-great-
grandparents are your ancestors.

breed (BREED)
A type of dog, or other animal.

canine (KAY-nine)
A member of the dog family. Canine is often written
as K-9.

cells (SELZ)
Very tiny parts of a living thing. Bones, muscles, skin,
hair, and every part of an animal are made of cells.

domesticated (duh-MESS-tuh-kate-id)
Tame and kept as a pet or farm animal.

endurance (en-DUR-uhnss)
The ability to keep going.

evolved (ee-VAHLVD)
Developed and changed gradually over many years.

olfactory epithelium
(ohl-FAK-tuh-ree ep-uh-THEE-lee-uhm)
A small area of tissue inside the nose. It contains millions of tiny receptors that capture smells.

predator (PRED-uh-tur)
An animal that hunts and eats other animals.

retina (RET-in-uh)
The back wall of an eyeball. Cells in the retina take the light that enters a person or animal's eyes and help turn it into the things that are seen.

tapetum (TAP ee-tuhm)
A layer of tissue in the eyes of some animals that helps them see in the dark.

Index

Read More

Gaines, Becky, with Gary Weitzman. *Everything Dogs (National Geographic Kids Everything).* Washington, DC: National Geographic (2012).

Owen, Ruth. *Goldendoodles (Designer Dogs).* New York: Rosen Publishing (2013).

Learn More Online

To learn more about dog senses and skills, go to
www.rubytuesdaybooks.com/superdog